Elephants around the World

The Animal Friends Books

Elephants around the World

by Sylvia A. Johnson

CAROLRHODA BOOKS

MINNEAPOLIS, MINNESOTA U S A

Revised English text by Sylvia A. Johnson. Original French text by Anne-Marie Pajot. Translation by Dyan Hammarberg. Photographs by Guy Dhuit, Jean-Louis Nou, and Rapho. Drawings by L'Enc Matte.

LIBRARY OF CONGRESS CATALOGING IN PUBLICATION DATA

Johnson, Sylvia A.
  Elephants around the world.

  (The Animal Friends Books)
  Original ed. published under title: Les elephants.
  SUMMARY: A young boy learns about elephants by visiting the zoo, attending the circus, and reading at home.

  1. Elephants — Juvenile literature. [1. Elephants] I. Pajot, Anne Marie. Les elephants. II. Dhuit, Guy. III. Nou, Jean Louis. IV. Rapho. V. Matte, L'Enc. VI. Title.

QL737.P98J62   599'.61   76-29438
ISBN 0-87614-075-4

First published in the United States of America 1977 by
Carolrhoda Books, Inc. All English language rights reserved.

Original edition published by Librairie A. Hatier, Paris,
France, under the title LES ELEPHANTS.
English text and drawings © 1977 Carolrhoda Books, Inc.
Photographs © 1969 Librairie A. Hatier.

Manufactured in the United States of America.
Published simultaneously in Canada by J. M. Dent & Sons
(Canada) Ltd., Don Mills, Ontario.

International Standard Book Number: 0-87614-075-4
Library of Congress Catalog Card Number: 76-29438

2 3 4 5 6 7 8 9 10 85 84 83 82 81 80 79

Of all the animals in our world, Frank likes elephants the best. He likes to read books about elephants and to look at pictures of elephants. When his class studied animals in school, Frank wrote a special report on elephants and where they live.

Now Frank is very excited because he is finally going to see some *real* elephants. Tomorrow, he and his family are going to visit the new zoo, and at the zoo, there are two real-live elephants.

The drive to the zoo doesn't take very long, but to Frank, it seems to last forever. Finally, the entrance to the zoo is in sight, and the noises of the animals can be heard clearly.

And there are the elephants, standing proudly in their enclosure. Frank runs up to the fence and stares as hard as he can. How big they are! Elephants never looked so *big* in the pictures he has seen. And he never knew that their tusks were so long and sharp, or their trunks so flexible— just like the body of a snake. Elephants are much more exciting in real life than they are in pictures.

Frank gets as close to the elephants as he can, but he doesn't feed them peanuts or candy, as people sometimes do. He knows that this is against the rules and that it isn't good for the elephants. Frank would like to climb up on the back of an elephant, but that is against the rules too. Someday, perhaps he will have a chance to visit the big zoo in Capitol City and to ride the elephants there. That zoo has special elephants just for children to ride.

After his day at the zoo, Frank is tired, but his mother and father have another surprise for him. The circus is in town, and they have tickets for it. Frank will be able to see more elephants!

The elephants at the circus are not just ordinary elephants. They have had special training, and they can do all kinds of tricks. Frank watches in amazement as some elephants roll on the ground, while others sit up on their hind legs.

Look at that! An elephant is standing with all four feet on a large ball. He balances himself on the ball just as easily as if he were standing on the ground. And on top of the elephant's head is a pretty girl, who smiles and waves at the people. Frank claps loudly to show his approval. His favorite animals are not only very large—they are also very smart.

After the circus is over, Frank is ready to go home and to bed. All night long, he dreams about elephants—elephants at the zoo, elephants in the circus, and, best of all, elephants in their own natural homes.

The next day, Frank gets out all his books about elephants and looks at them once again. In the books are pictures of elephants in their homes on the other side of the world.

Some elephants live in the far-away land of Africa. Their homes are on the African *savannas,* dry plains covered with grass and dotted with a few trees. Frank reads in his book that African elephants live in groups, or herds. In a herd, there are grown-up male and female elephants and young elephants of different ages. Some of the young elephants are only babies. They stay close to the mother elephants and often hold onto their mothers' tails with their trunks.

The leader of an elephant herd is usually an old female elephant. The other members of the herd follow her as she wanders over the savanna. Elephants sometimes travel for great distances when they are searching for water and food. They move in single file, and they make very little noise, despite their large size. Their average speed is about six miles (10 kilometers) an hour, but they can move much faster if they have to.

Frank is so busy reading about elephants that he doesn't even realize he has a visitor. His cousin Nora has come to spend the afternoon. Soon, both Frank and Nora have their heads bent over the elephant books.

"Here is a picture of an African elephant," Frank tells Nora. "See how big its ears are. And this elephant with small ears is an Asian elephant. Asian elephants live in the forests of India, Thailand, and other countries in southeast Asia. They are smaller than African elephants. Another way that you can tell Asian elephants from African elephants is by looking at their foreheads. African elephants have smooth foreheads, but the foreheads of Asian elephants are bumpy."

Of course, both kinds of elephants have those amazing trunks. An elephant's trunk serves not only as a nose but also as a kind of hand. Elephants can use their trunks to pick up something as small as a piece of fruit or as large as a log. They can also fill their trunks with water and squirt the water into their mouths. This is how elephants drink.

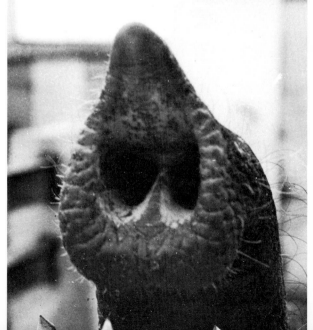

"What do elephants eat?" Nora wonders. "Plants," answers Frank. "Lots and lots of plants. Wild elephants spend most of their time searching for food and eating. They can eat as much as 600 pounds (270 kilograms) of grass and leaves in one day. They often use their trunks to pick up their food and to put it into their mouths. When elephants eat, they don't have very good manners. Sometimes an elephant will knock down a whole tree just to get the tender leaves at the top."

"Elephants sure have an easy life," says Nora, "eating all day long!"

"Some elephants do more than just eat," Frank tells her. "Asian elephants work hard, helping people to lift and carry things."

Frank goes on to explain that such elephants are captured when they are young. Then they are trained to follow the orders given by men who ride on their backs. The elephant riders tell the elephants what to do by giving signals with their legs and feet.

"Look, Nora, here is a picture of an elephant moving a heavy rock. And this elephant is lifting a big log and holding it on his tusks. Elephants often work in the forests of Asia. They can do some kinds of jobs that even machines can't do."

After a hard day's work, Asian elephants hurry to the river to take a bath. They lie down in the water, and their drivers scrub them with big brushes. Like all elephants, Asian elephants love water. They love to wade in it and to swim in it—elephants are very good swimmers. The animals also enjoy showering themselves with water sucked up into their trunks.

Splashing in the river helps elephants to cool off in the heat, and it also helps to get rid of biting insects. Even though elephants have thick skins, they are bothered by insect bites. When there is no water for them to bathe in, elephants will often roll in mud or sand to drive away insects.

"Elephants really are wonderful animals," Nora says to Frank. "They can do so many kinds of things."

"The people of Asia think that elephants are wonderful too," Frank replies. "In some Asian countries, elephants take part in celebrations and religious festivals. They march in parades wearing beautiful decorations made of gold and jewels. On their backs, they carry important people and images of the gods. This book has a picture of an elephant decorated for a festival. Its skin is painted with bright-colored flowers. When the festival is over, the paint will be washed off and the elephant's skin will be dark grey, just like always."

"I *like* elephants," Nora says, as Frank closes his book and puts it on the shelf. "From now on, they are going to be my favorite animals, too!"

DO YOU KNOW . . .

- the name for a male elephant?

- how a baby elephant drinks its mother's milk?

- what a *shovel-tusker* is?

TO FIND THE ANSWERS TO THESE QUESTIONS, TURN THE PAGE 👉

FACTS ABOUT ELEPHANTS

Elephants are the largest land animals in the world. A male African elephant is usually about 11½ feet (3.5 meters) tall at the shoulder and weighs around 14,000 pounds (6,350 kilograms). A male Asian elephant is about 9 feet (2.7 meters) tall and weighs around 12,000 pounds (5,400 kilograms). The females of both species are smaller than the males.

A male elephant is called a *bull*. Female elephants are known as *cows*. Baby elephants are called *calves*.

A baby elephant weighs about 200 pounds (91 kilograms) at birth. The calf will drink its mother's milk until it is three or four years old. When a young elephant nurses, it curls its trunk back over its head and raises its mouth to its mother's breasts. A female elephant has two breasts, located between her front legs.

The long tusks that extend out from an elephant's mouth are actually two of the animal's teeth. These two teeth are called *incisors* (in-SI-zuhrs). Elephants also have four grinding teeth, or *molars,* inside their mouths. The molars are used to chew food.

Today, many African and Asian elephants live in parks and protected areas, where they are safe from human hunters. But elephants need such big areas to live in that it is hard to find enough space for them. In some parks in Africa, the plants and trees are being destroyed because of the large numbers of elephants feeding on them.

In the distant past, there were many relatives of the elephant that roamed the earth. One was the *mastodon* (MASS-tuh-dahn), a large animal that lived in North America until about 8,000 years ago. The *shovel-tusker* was a strange kind of mastodon with a lower jaw shaped like a shovel. Modern elephants are probably descended from the *mammoth,* a huge beast that lived on the earth at the same time as prehistoric humans.

Shovel-Tusker

Mastodon

Wooly Mammoth

The Animal Friends Books

Clover the CALF
Jessie the CHICKEN
Ali the DESERT FOX
Splash the DOLPHIN
Dolly the DONKEY
Downy the DUCKLING
ELEPHANTS around the World
Tippy the FOX TERRIER
Marigold the GOLDFISH
Polly the GUINEA PIG
Winslow the HAMSTER
Figaro the HORSE

Rusty the IRISH SETTER
Boots the KITTEN
Penny and Pete the LAMBS
The LIONS of Africa
Mandy the MONKEY
Lorito the PARROT
Curly the PIGLET
Whiskers the RABBIT
Shelley the SEA GULL
Penelope the TORTOISE
Sprig the TREE FROG
Tanya the TURTLE DOVE

Additional titles in preparation

CAROLRHODA BOOKS
241 FIRST AVENUE NORTH — MINNEAPOLIS, MINNESOTA 55401

*Published in memory of Carolrhoda Locketz Rozell,
Who loved to bring children and books together*

Please write for a complete catalogue